antoinette portis

Hey, Water!

Scallywag Press Ltd

LONDON

Hey, Water!

A book to share from
Scallywag Press

Thanks to the United States Geological Survey for their help.

First published in Great Britain in 2020 by Scallywag Press Ltd,
10 Sutherland Row, London SW1V 4JT
This paperback edition published in 2021

Originally published in the USA as a Neal Porter Book by Holiday House Publishing, Inc., New York

Printed on FSC paper in China by Toppan Leefung

001

British Library Cataloguing in Publication Data available

ISBN 978-1-912650-60-6

Hey, water! I know you!
You're all around.

tap

sprinkler

You spray up

and down.

shower

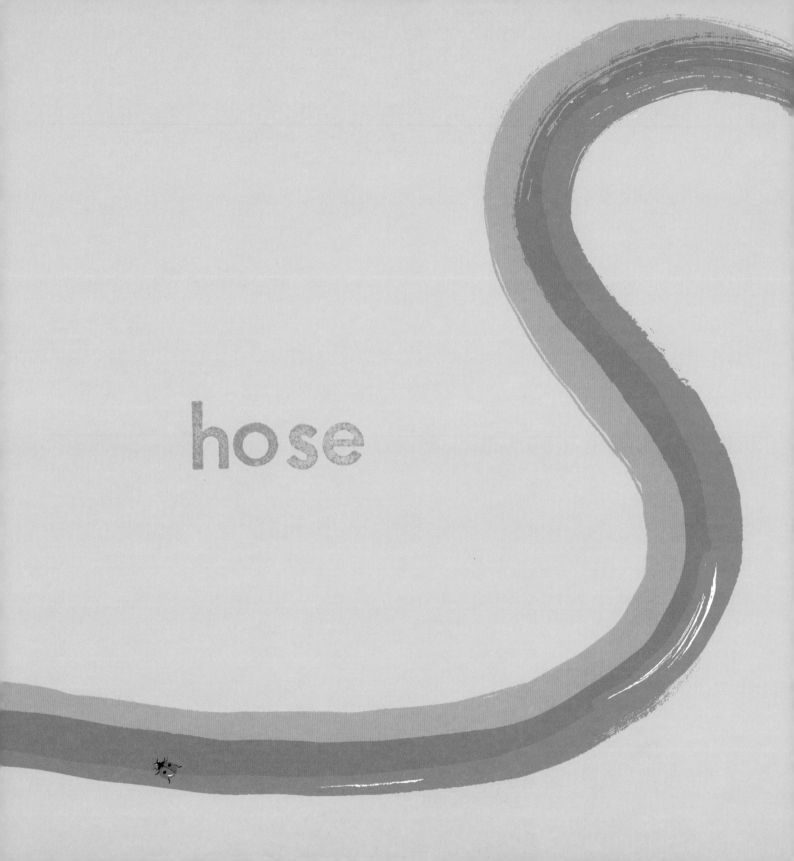

hose

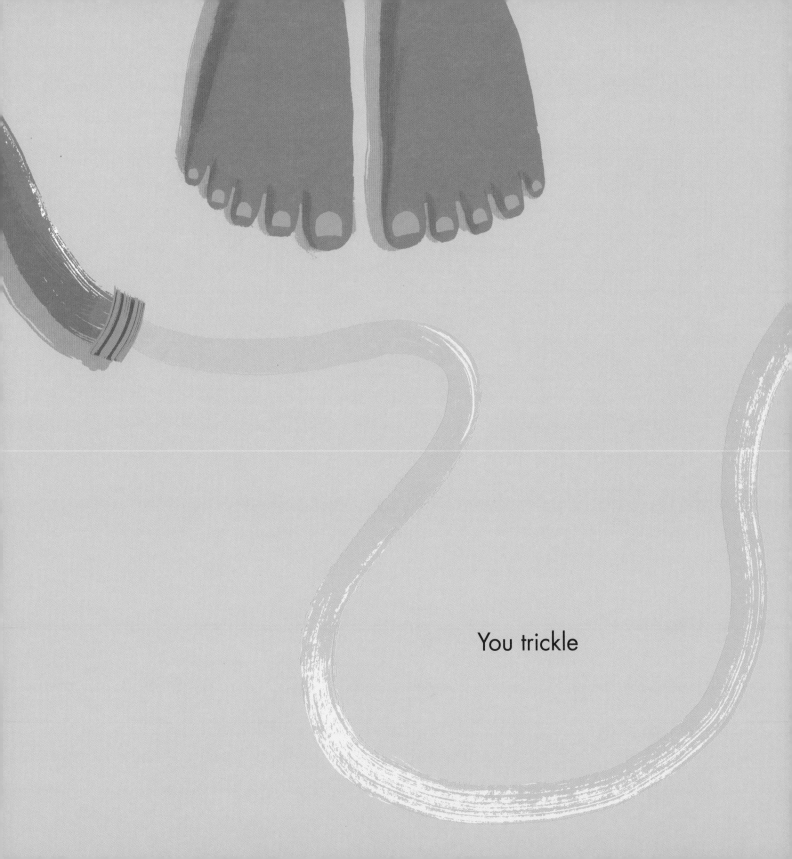

You trickle

and gurgle

stream

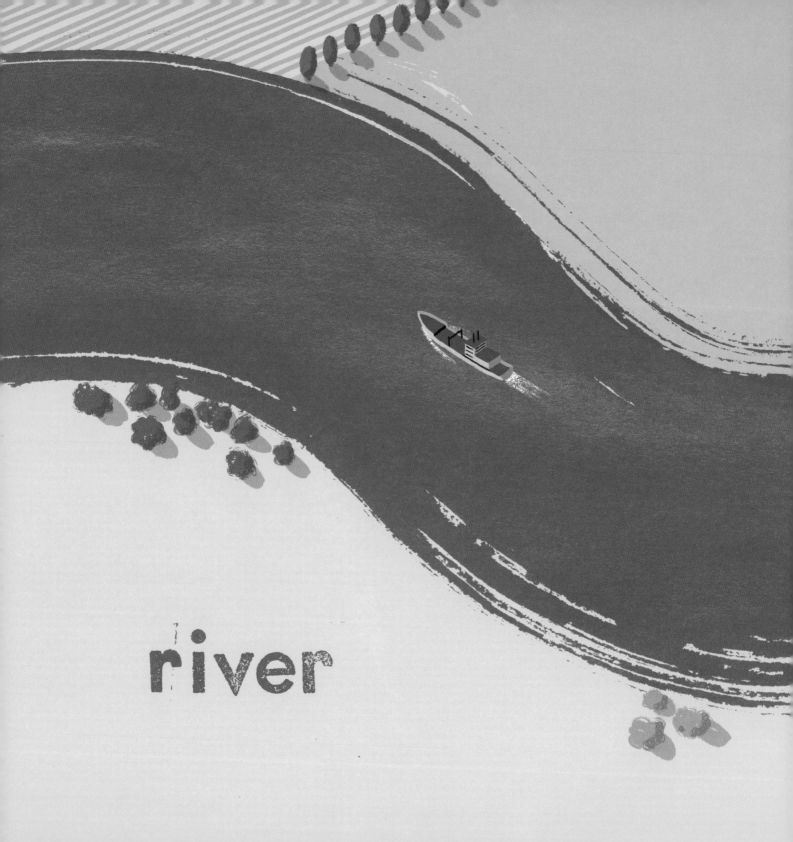

river

and rush towards the sea.

You cover most of the earth—
salty, surging, and mysterious.

ocean

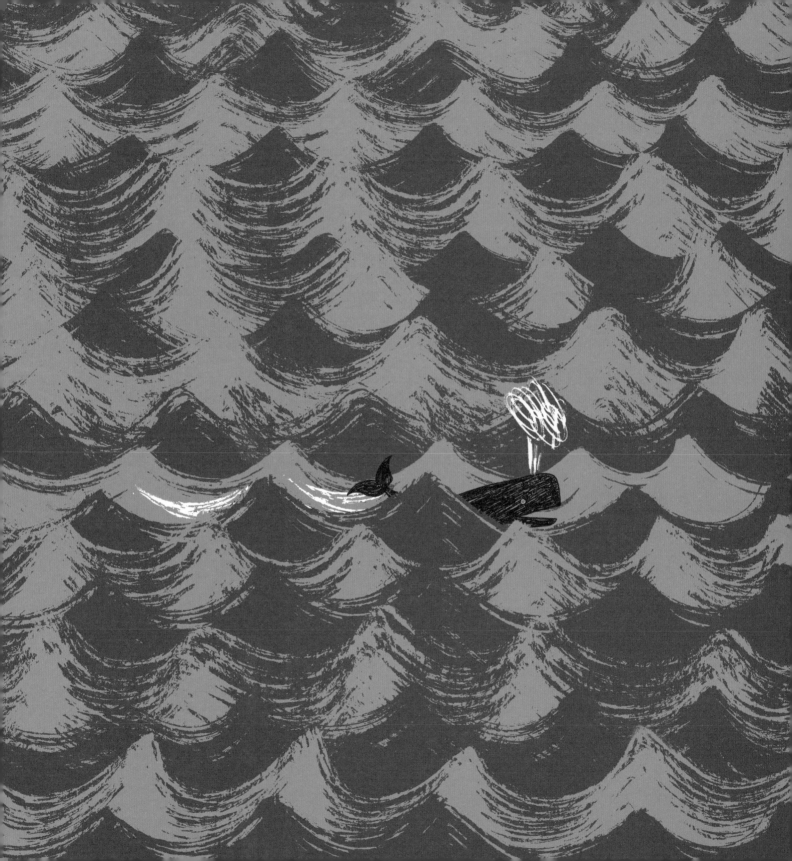

Sometimes you lie, quiet and calm,

lake

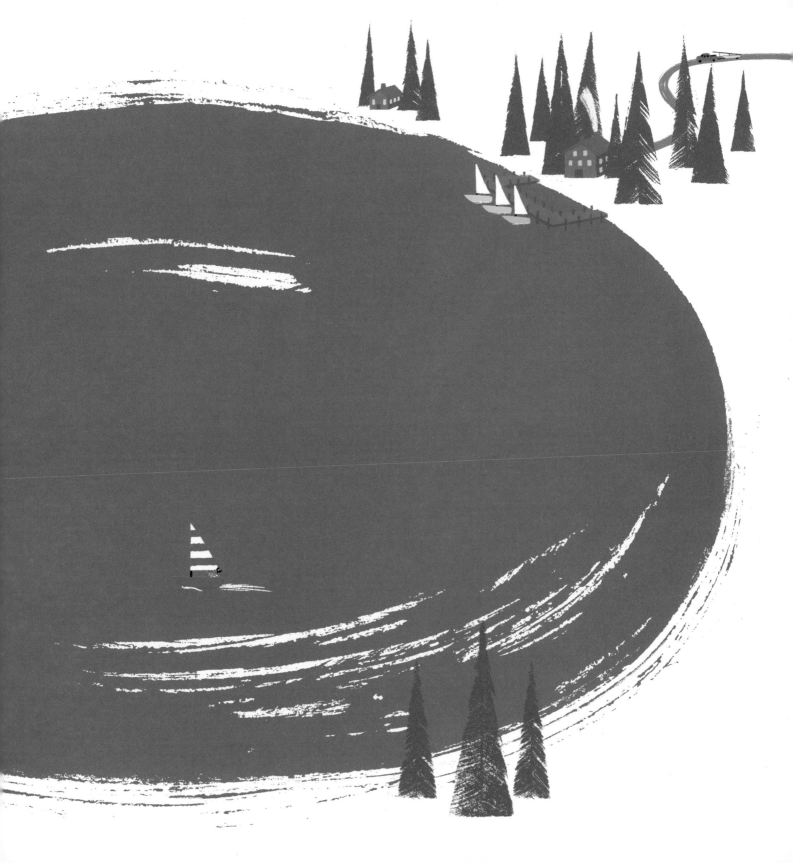

so we can splash and play
and yell in you.

pool

I stomp in you and
scatter droplets everywhere.

In the morning, you wink at me from blades of grass.

dewdrop

Sometimes you slide down my cheek without a sound.

tear

rain

Sometimes you roar and pour.

Water, even when you try to fool me, I know you.

You blast and huff.

You whistle and puff.

steam

You hide in the air and drift.

cloud

You drift in the air and hide

fog

the world.

Sometimes you freeze hard as a rock—

ice cube

iceberg

a rock that floats,

or a rock we can skate on.

rink

Water, you're a part of every living thing.

When I'm thirsty, there you are.

bathtub

Hey, water,
thank you !

water forms

liquid

Nearly three-quarters of Earth's surface (70%) is covered in liquid water, and water makes up three-quarters of a baby's body. Water is needed for life and takes many forms beyond the water we drink. Clouds and fog are made of tiny floating water droplets; when these droplets clump together and get too heavy to float, they fall as rain.

solid

When water is cooled it freezes into a solid. Solid water appears as tiny crystalline snowflakes, hail, ice cubes, or huge floating icebergs.

gas

When water is heated, it turns into an invisible gas called water vapour. Rain puddles disappear as the sun's warmth slowly changes liquid water into vapour. You can see steam shooting out of a kettle. This isn't water vapour, but a mist made of tiny hot water droplets suspended in the air.

Steam is tiny drops of hot water.

Water vapour is invisible. It's in the air!

conserving water

We can turn on a tap to get clean drinking water, but around the world, some people must walk miles every day to get water to drink, wash, cook and grow food.

We can't drink salty sea water or grow plants with it. We need fresh water, but it only makes up 3% of the world's water supply. We can't drink or use most of the world's fresh water, because it is frozen in glaciers and polar ice caps.

We use fresh water faster than it falls as rain or snow, while a warming climate is drying up lakes and rivers. If we don't use our fresh water more carefully, some living things won't have enough water to survive.

the water cycle

condensation
Cold air causes water vapour to turn back into liquid droplets.

precipitation
Water falls to the ground as liquid or solid.

evaporation
The sun's heat turns liquid into vapour that rises up into the air.

collection
Water runs downhill and collects in rivers and lakes, as well as seeps down into the ground.

This cycle has repeated over and over again for millions of years.

fun with water

Play and learn about water

cleaning water

- Put a paper towel in a funnel and insert the funnel into a plastic bottle.
- Pour some muddy water over the towel, so it drips through the funnel.
- Is the water inside the bottle cleaner now?
- What's left behind on the towel? Why?

Water must be clean so it's safe to drink.

living water

- Put cotton wool on a saucer and sprinkle it with cress seeds.
- Pour some water over the seeds.
- Put cotton wool and cress seeds on another saucer, but don't water these seeds.
- Wait a few days. Which seeds begin to sprout? Why?

All living things need water to survive.

watching water

- Put an ice cube in a bowl and leave it outside on a sunny day.
- What happens to the ice? Why?
- Leave the bowl out in the sunshine.
- What happens to the water in the bowl? Why?

Ice is frozen water. If water is heated, it turns into invisible water vapour.

saving water

- Give six friends empty cups to hold and ask them to stand in a line.
- Fill your cup with water and mark the water level. Empty it into the first cup.
- Ask your friends to pass the water along the line, emptying from cup to cup.
- Pour the water back into your cup. Check the level – have you lost any water? Why?

Water is precious, so we must all try hard to look after it.

true or false?

Read this book to find the answers

1. **Most of the Earth is dry land.** True or false?

2. **Water is in every living thing.** True or false?

3. **The sea flows into rivers.** True or false?

4. **Water is in clouds and fog.** True or false?

5. **Icebergs are too big to float.** True or false?

5) FALSE: Icebergs are huge blocks of floating ice.

4) TRUE: Water hides in the air, both in clouds and fog.

3) FALSE: Rivers rush towards the sea.

2) TRUE: Water is a part of all the plants and animals on Earth, including you!

1) FALSE: Water covers most of the Earth.

Hey, Water!

The perfect book for any budding scientist or artist or scientist-artist!
Irish Independent

A clever and joyful celebration of the science and language of water,
this is a superb example of an information text, ostensibly for younger
children, but with multi-age and multi-curriculum uses.
A model of writing and the effective use of figurative language -
perfect for vocabulary building for the youngest child.
A really well thought out and brilliantly executed early science
picture book that deserves a place in every school.
LoveReading4Schools

This delightful non-fiction book is one to be brought out repeatedly
as your child reaches new stages of learning.
INIS magazine

Skilfully introduces the concept of one element, water, being found
in different forms, different states and from different sources.
The whole book presents a science topic from a young child's perspective
and combines playfulness and learning in an appealing way.
This would be an excellent addition to school, public and family libraries as
it combines themes of science and conservation with striking design
and use of colour to appeal to a range of ages.
Books for Keeps

Antoinette Portis is also the author and illustrator of
A New Green Day, nominated for the *Kate Greenaway Medal*, 2021

Find out more at www.scallywagpress.com